CREDIT REPAIR SECRETS

(FROM "THE CREDIT DOCTOR")

BY DANIEL ROSEN

First Edition 2009

For more information about the author
and our credit repair software products,
visit www.credit-aid.com

TABLE OF CONTENTS

INTRODUCTION FROM "THE CREDIT DOCTOR"

The credit reporting system in America is designed to keep people poor. Once you fall behind, it's becomes impossible to recover. This is no accident.

If you're late on a payment, they can raise your interest rate to 30% or higher, making it impossible to pay off...and lowering your credit score. This effects the interest rates on your other accounts and your problems start to multiply. This is how banks get richer.

There is something you can do. You do have the right to dispute negative items on your credit reports. Even accurate items can often be removed. You just need to know the rules.

Here in this booklet are the basic tools needed to repair your credit and dispute and negotiate away negative items.

For more information about the nuts and bolts of credit repair, and to try out our popular credit repair software, please visit our web site at www.credit-aid.com.

Sincerely

Daniel Rosen
"The Credit Doctor"
Founder and CEO of Credit-Aid Software
www.credit-aid.com

WHAT A LOW CREDIT SCORE REALLY COSTS YOU

Do you know what a low credit score really costs you? Your monthly payments can be over 40% higher with a low score!

A higher credit score can save you an enormous amount of money because it usually means a lower mortgage interest rate. It also can mean the difference between qualifying for a loan or not.

According to Fair Isaac, lenders would probably demand a 9.8 percent interest rate on a $300,000, 30-year fixed mortgage for a borrower with a credit score between 500 and 579. That would translate into a $2,585 monthly payment for principal and interest. But a borrower with a score between 760 and 850 seeking the same loan would qualify for about a 6 percent rate that would cost just $1,796 a month for principal and interest. That savings of $789 each month would total $284,040 over 30 years!

Do you know what your credit score really costs you over the life of a loan? If your score is above 720 you should have no trouble qualifying for a low rate loan. But the lower your score is the more difficult it will be to qualify, and the higher the interest will be. Your monthly payments can be over 40% higher with a low score!

Here is a chart that illustrates the effect a low credit score can cost you over the life of a loan:

YOUR CREDIT SCORE	*ADDITIONAL COST TO YOU
720+	$0
700-719	$7,000
675-699	$30,100
620-674	$86,450
560-619	$143,640
500-559	$287,200

*Based on a 30 year $200K loan @ 5.6% interest

How your FICO (credit) score directly affects your Interest Rate:

FICO stands for Fair, Issac & Co. They're the folks who created the mathematical formula used to calculate what is commonly called the FICO score. This three-digit number is a big determinant in whether or not you get a mortgage or any other type of loan. FICO helps banks, credit card issuers, auto loan companies and other lenders decide if you're a good credit risk. It also makes a difference in the interest rate you're offered. Obviously, the higher your score, the more likely you'll be approved for a mortgage (and one with a low rate).

YOUR CREDIT SCORE	*INTEREST RATE
720+	6.089%
700-719	6.214%
675-699	6.751%
620-674	7.901%
560-619	8.531%
500-559	9.289%

*Based upon recent rates

As you can see, a credit score of 720 or higher is the magic number to hit.

It's as simple as this:

A better credit report will raise your credit score. A higher credit score will get you a lower interest rate. The lower your interest rate, the more money you will save.

You can repair your Credit quickly. You can have negative misinformation wiped away from your reports, you can negotiate with creditors to remove negative postings and lower your payments, and you can raise your credit score higher so you can get the loan that you want at the low interest rated you deserve. All it takes is perseverance, a positive attitude and knowledge. You're reading these tips and that's good positive start.

Just remember: If every single day you do at least one thing to better your credit, you will generate momentum to bring you closer to your goal.

I hope you enjoy this booklet and find it useful! Good luck to you on your journey to better credit

— Credit Doctor

YOUR CREDIT REPORTS

A credit report is the equivalent of a consumer's financial report card. It details your credit history as it has been reported to the credit reporting agency by the lenders who've given you credit. Your credit report lists the types of credit you use, the amount of time your accounts have been open, and if you pay your bills on time.

Your credit report is used by many different companies to make decisions about you. Credit card companies, banks, mortgage companies, auto loan and insurance companies, also landlords and employers check credit reports to check on your credit history. Why? They know that if you were responsible in the past, you are likely to be responsible in the future (and vice versa).

CREDIT SCORING

"Credit scoring" of is a system creditors use to help determine whether to give you credit, and how much to charge you for it. When you apply for credit, the creditor or lender will often request your report (or credit score) from one of the big three bureaus (Equifax, Experian or Trans-Union). In some instances, however (such as when applying for a Mortgage), the broker or lender will pull reports from all three. These Bureaus grade your "credit worthiness" by calculating your credit history against a system called the Fair Isaac Model. Fair Isaac uses a variety of factors to determine your score, such as; your bill-paying history, the number and type of accounts you have, late payments, collection actions, outstanding debt, and the age of your accounts.

The final outcome of those calculations is referred to as your FICO® score. FICO® scores range from 300 to 850, but the majority of scores fall between the 600s and 700s. Higher scores indicate a lower credit risk. A FICO® score above 700 will get you a very good mortgage rate. A score above 720 will get you an excellent rate. A score below 700 will make it very difficult for you, and definitely should be worked on.

Correcting mistakes on a credit report in order to repair an undesirable credit score takes time. It's your responsibility to correct mistakes that may appear in your credit report. To do this, you must regularly obtain copies of your credit reports, and contact each of the big three credit reporting bureaus to correct any misinformation.

ORDERING COPIES OF YOUR CREDIT REPORTS

The three nationwide consumer reporting companies now use one website, one toll-free telephone number, and one mailing address for consumers to order their free annual report. To order, visit www.annualcreditreport.com , call 1-877-322-8228, or complete an Annual Credit Report Request Form and mail it to: Annual Credit Report Request Service, P.O. Box 105281, Atlanta, GA 30348-5281. You can print it from www.ftc.gov/credit . You may order your free annual reports from each of the consumer reporting companies at the same time, or you can order from only one or two. The law allows you to order one free copy from each of the nationwide consumer reporting companies every 12 months.

You need to provide your name, address, Social Security number, and date of birth. If you have moved in the last two years, you may have to provide your previous address. To maintain the security of your file, each nationwide consumer reporting company may ask you for some information that only you would know, like the amount of your monthly mortgage payment. Each company may ask you for different information because the information each has in your file may come from different sources.

www.annualcreditreport.com is the only authorized online source for your free annual credit report from the three nationwide consumer reporting companies. Neither the website nor the companies will call you first to ask for personal information or send you an email asking for personal information. If you get a phone call or an email — or see a pop-up ad — claiming it's from www.annualcreditreport.com (or any of the three nationwide consumer reporting companies), it's probably a scam. Don't reply or click on any link in the message. Instead, forward any email that claims to be from www.annualcreditreport.com (or any of the three consumer reporting companies) to spam@uce.gov , the FTC's database of deceptive spam.

There are also other circumstances which will allow you to receive free credit history reports. Under federal law, you're entitled to a free report if a company takes adverse action against you, such as denying your application for credit, insurance, or employment, and you ask for your report within 60 days of receiving notice of the action. The notice will give you the name, address, and phone number of the consumer reporting company. You're also entitled to one free report per year if you're unemployed and plan to look for a job within 60 days; if you're on welfare; or if your report is inaccurate because of fraud or identity theft. Otherwise, any of the three consumer reporting companies may charge you up to $10.00 for another copy of your report within a 12-month period.

To buy copies of your credit history report, contact:

Equifax
800-685-1111
www.equifax.com

Experian
888-EXPERIAN (397-3742)
www.experian.com

Trans Union
800-916-8800
www.transunion.com

Under state law, consumers in Colorado, Georgia, Maine, Maryland, Massachusetts, New Jersey, and Vermont already have free access to their credit reports.

For more information, see "Your Access to Free Credit Reports" at www.ftc.gov/credit .

REVIEWING YOUR CREDIT REPORTS

Recent studies by a Public Interest Research Group found that over 70% of credit reports contain errors. Incorrect information in your credit file lowers your credit score. As the result you get a higher interest rate when you: take a loan, open a new credit card account, lease a car, etc. 29% of the credit reports in this study contained even more serious errors that could result in the denial of credit. These errors included false delinquencies, public records, judgments and credit accounts that did not belong to the consumer. Sometimes these errors are the work of sloppy data entry, but it is also often due to the ever growing epidemic of identity theft.

Since your Credit Reports are used to determine IF you are to be given credit (and what rates you will be charged), it is in your best interest to examine your reports carefully, correct inaccurate information and make every effort to remove ALL Unfavorable information. If you see problems on your report, such as an unpaid bill that you simply forgot about, act right away to resolve the debt. Then ask that creditor to send a letter to the credit reporting agencies stating that the matter has been resolved.

Check for accounts you didn't open, charges you haven't made, and delinquencies you didn't cause. If you suspect fraud on one of your reports, contact that credit bureau IMMEDIATELY. Explain the situation and ask them to place a fraud alert on your file. Also report the fraud to the police.

Your credit reports follow you throughout your life and can help you greatly -- or hurt you. Review them carefully!

HOW TO READ YOUR CREDIT REPORTS

The bulk of the report will be filled with credit information showing the following:

1). Identification Information

The first thing listed will be your name, date of birth and Social Security number. These are used for identification. Employment information may also be listed. As well as current and past addresses, spouse's name (if you're married) and date of birth are also listed for further identification.

2). Public Record Information

Data from federal, state or county court records. Bankruptcies, liens or judgments and other types of claims. The information listed will be; Date filed, court case number, amount, status and date settled.

3). Collection Agency Information

A collection is an account that has been turned over to a collection agency by one of your creditors because you have not paid the account as agreed. Listed here are; collector's name, originating creditor/client, original amount, balance due and account number.

4). Credit Information

This section makes up the bulk of the report. It will include mortgage, installment, revolving, other, open and closed accounts. It will also list accounts in good standing, accounts currently past due, negative account history, merchant/creditor name, subscriber number, account number, date opened, date closed, current balance, highest credit limit, highest amount of credit used, and your repayment history. Your repayment history is shown as a string of numbers showing your payment history.

With each credit account, you will see listed the account's status and history. They are generally marked as follows;

- ✓ Current Account - "Account Open" or "Closed in Good Standing"

- ✓ Closed Account - Credit Account Closed

- ✓ Paid Account - Closed Account or Zero Balance

- ✓ Credit Account Reinstated - Previously Closed Account Now Available for use

- ✓ Foreclosure - Collateral sold to collect Defaulted Mortgage

- ✓ Collection Account - Credit Account Assigned to Collection Agency

- ✓ Inquiry - your credit information was requested by this Company or Creditor

5). Inquiries that display

All authorized and legitimate requests to see your credit history.

6). Inquiries that DO NOT display

These inquiries are displayed only to you and are not considered when tabulating your credit score. Examples of this inquiry type include a pre-approved offer of credit, insurance or periodic account reviews by an existing creditor.

7). Consumer Statements

If for some reason you cannot prove that a negative item is an error or if you are having a disagreement with a certain creditor, you have the right to tell your side of the story in 100 words or less. This statement will be ADDED to your report.

WHAT TO LOOK FOR IN YOUR CREDIT REPORTS

Credit Reports seem rather cryptic at first, but once you see how they are laid out they will start to make sense. These are the important things to examine:

1. Make sure your personal Information is correct.

2. Make sure your accounts are listed correctly.

3. Make sure your credit lines are listed correctly (see next chapter).

4. Make sure your balances are listed correctly.

5. If you closed an account, it should say "Account closed BY CONSUMER."

MAKE SURE YOUR CREDIT REPORTS CONTAIN THE PROPER CREDIT LIMITS. BANKS ARE GETTING SNEAKY!

Some creditors and lenders do not report consumer credit limits. Instead they will only post the highest balance you have ever carried. Keeping proper credit limit information out of your file is not always an innocent oversight. It's often done purposely by a bank to make you look less attractive to their competitors, so they won't send you pre-approved offers. Worst of all, it lowers your credit score!

Capital One is famous for this sneaky tactic: Instead of reporting customers' proper credit limits, they often only report the highest balance carried, which give the appearance that you are closer to maxing out your card than you really are (which is bad for your credit score). Interestingly, we are told that FICO scores no longer use this information from Capital One when computing credit scores, but you may want to go through your credit report with a fine tooth comb to make sure that none of your other accounts are listed with inaccurate credit limits. Generally speaking, the more available credit you have, the better you look on your credit report.

If you find that a lender is not listing the proper credit line on your account, and it's not Capital One, you might want to call and ask them to report the right amount. Sometimes, it is their company policy not to report, but you certainly can try.

STATING YOUR DISPUTE

Make certain that all information is current and accurate, including the Personal Identification information (address, social security, etc...). If you find an error (for example, a loan that you have PAID OFF is still listed as outstanding), tell the Credit Bureau (in writing) EXACTLY what the mistake is, and explain the way that the information SHOULD be listed. For example, "My Loan to Bank of Fred is NOT outstanding. It was paid in full on 02/14/2009." Send photocopies along with all the necessary information to backup your claim.

After you have done this send it to the credit bureau by "CERTIFIED MAIL." When the credit bureau receives your report and the information in question, they are required to investigate and ADVISE YOU of the results of their investigation. They must do this Free of charge.

Anytime that you are denied credit you have the right to know why. If you are turned down for a credit account at a store, you will receive a statement from the store stating that you were denied credit and their reason why. If the store based their decision on your credit history, they must provide you with the name and address of the agency that reported it.

If for some reason you cannot prove that a negative item is an error or if you are having a disagreement with a certain creditor, you have the right to tell your side of the story in 100 words or less. This statement will be ADDED to your report.

When correcting items on your credit report, you have the right to demand that the credit bureau send corrected copies of your report to all creditors who have received the incorrect reports for the past six months. Note: Credit bureaus will not do this automatically! They will only do it if you ask. So make sure you ask. It's your right!

SAMPLE DISPUTE LETTER

Here is a sample letter with sample dispute items. Use the ones you need and delete the rest.

Your Name
Your Address
City, State Zip
Your Date of Birth:
Social Security Number:
Credit Report Number: _____

Credit Bureau Name
Credit Bureau Address
City, State Zip

Today's Date

Re: Letter to Remove Inaccurate Credit Information – Credit Report #_____

To Whom It May Concern:

I received a copy of my credit report and found the following item(s) to be errors. See the attached copy of my credit report, the errors have been highlighted.

Here as follows are items in error:

Incorrect Personal Information:

XXXXXXXXXXXXXXXX

Correct Personal Information:

XXXXXXXXXXXXX

The following accounts below are not mine:

Creditor's Name
Account Number
Explanation:

The account status is incorrect for the following accounts:

Creditor's Name
Account Number
Correct Status:

The following information is outdated. I would like it removed from my credit history report:

Creditor's Name
Account Number
Date of Last Activity

The following inquiries are more than two years old and I would like them removed:

Creditor's Name
Date of Inquiry

These inquiries below were not authorized:

Creditor's Name
Date of Inquiry

Explanation

The following accounts were closed by me and should state that:

Creditor's Name
Account Number

Other information I would like changed:

Explanation

By the provisions of the Fair Credit Reporting Act, I demand that these items be investigated and removed from my report.

It is my understanding that you will recheck these items with the creditor who has posted them. Please remove any information that the creditor cannot verify.

I understand that under 15 U.S.C. Sec. 1681i(a), you must complete this reinvestigation within 30 days of receipt of this letter. Please send an updated copy of my credit report to the above address. According to the act, there shall be no charge for this updated report. I also request that you please send notices of corrections to anyone who received my credit report in the past six months.

Thank you time and help in this matter.

Sincerely,

_____

[Signature]

Make sure you send this letter by certified mail. Enclose a copy of the credit report containing the items you are disputing. It may also help to circle the items. Also include copies (not originals) of any paperwork you may have that validates your claims.

DEALING WITH NEGATIVE (BUT CORRECT) INFORMATION ON YOUR REPORT (AND COLLECTION AGENCIES)

Despite popular belief, it is often possible to negotiate removal of negative items on your credit reports posted by creditors. In some cases, you might not even have to pay them the full amount owed*. The important thing is to be positive, be patient and get in contact with them to try to work out a deal.

If you've ignored (or never received) a creditor's bills or phone calls, or if you failed to keep up with payments, your bill may be turned over to a collection agency. Keep in mind that collection agencies are hired by the creditor and their only goal is to collect the money owed (or as much of it as they can) as quickly as possible. For their efforts, they are paid a percentage of what they collect.

If you feel that the amount in question is being billed in error, you have the right to ask for proof and verification of the charges. If the charges are indeed yours it may be in your best interest to negotiate with the collection agency. You may be able to negotiate payment of the total sum (or even a partial amount) in return for their removing their negative marks on your Credit History Report. You might be able to settle on paying a portion of your debt, or you might be able to work out a payment installment plan with them. Many of the Creditor letters in the STOREROOM can be used with collection agencies for these situations. Whatever deal you make with them, be sure that you have it all in writing prior to paying them.

Collection agencies can be very aggressive when it comes to collecting money. Remember that you have rights. You have the right to ask a collection agency stop contacting you, especially if you feel harassed. Use these letters below to give yourself breathing room while working through your plan to reorganize your finances.

*See the letters in the Storeroom section.

SEVEN STEPS TO BOOST YOUR FICO SCORE

1. **Correct all inaccuracies on your Credit Report.**

   Go through your credit reports very carefully. Especially look for; late payments, charge-offs, collections or other negative items that aren't yours, accounts listed as "settled," "paid derogatory," "paid charge-off" or anything other than "current" or "paid as agreed" if you paid on time and in full, accounts that are still listed as unpaid that were included in a bankruptcy, negative items older than seven years (10 in the case of bankruptcy) that should have automatically fallen off your report (you must be careful with this last one, because sometimes scores actually go down when bad items fall off your report. It's a quirk in the FICO credit-scoring software, and the potential effect of eliminating old negative items is difficult to predict in advance). Also make sure you don't have duplicate collection notices listed. For example; if you have an account that has gone to collections, the original creditor may list the debt, as well as the collection agency. Any duplicates must be removed!

2. **Make sure that your proper credit lines are posted on your Credit Reports.**

   Often, in an effort to make you less desirable to their competitors, some creditors will not post your proper credit line. Showing less available credit can negatively impact your credit score. If you see this happening on your credit report, you have a right to complain and bring this to their attention. If you have bankruptcies that should be showing a zero balance...make sure they show a zero balance! Very often the creditor will not report a "bankruptcy charge-off" as a zero balance until it's been disputed.

3. **If you have any negative marks on your credit report, negotiate with the creditor/lender to remove it.**

   If you are a long time customer and it's something simple like a one-time late payment, a creditor will often wipe it away to keep you as a loyal customer. If you have a serious negative mark (such as a long overdue bill that has gone to collections), always negotiate a payment in exchange for removal of the negative item. Always make sure you have this agreement with them in writing. Do not pay off a bill that has gone to collections unless the creditor agrees in writing that they will remove the derogatory item from your credit report. This is important; when speaking with the creditor or collection agency about a debt that has gone to collections, do not admit that the debt is yours. Admission of debt can restart the statute of limitations, and may enable the creditor to sue you. You are also less likely to be able to negotiate a letter of deletion if you admit that this debt is yours. Simply say "I'm calling about account number _____" instead of "I'm calling about my past due debt."

4. **Pay all credit cards and any revolving credit down to below 30% of the available credit line.**

   The scoring system wants to make sure you aren't overextended, but at the same time, they want to see that you do indeed use your credit. 30% of the available credit line seems to be the magic "balance vs. credit line" ratio to have. For example; if you have a credit card with a $10,000 credit line, make sure that never more than $3000 (even if you pay your account off in full each month). If your balances are higher than 30% of the available credit line, pay them down. Here is another thing you can try; ask your long time creditors if they will raise your credit line without checking your FICO score or your credit report. Tell them that you're shopping for a house and you can't afford to have any hits on your credit report. Many will not but some will.

5. **Do not close your old credit card accounts.**

Old established accounts show your history, and tell about your stability and paying habits. If you have old credit card accounts that you want to stop using, just cut up the cards or keep them in a drawer, but keep the accounts open.

6. **Avoid applying for new credit.**

Each time you apply for new credit, your credit report gets checked. New credit cards will not help your credit score and a credit account less than one year old may hurt your credit score. Use your cards and credit as little as possible until the next credit scoring.

7. **Have at least three revolving credit lines and one active (or paid) installment loan listed on your Credit Report.**

The scoring system wants to see that you maintain a variety of credit accounts. It also wants to see that you have 3 revolving credit lines. If you do not have three active credit cards, you might want to open some (but keep in mind that if you do, you will need to wait some time before rescoring). If you have poor credit and are not approved for a typical credit card, you might want to set up a "secured credit card" account. This means that you will have to make a deposit that is equal or more than your limit, which guarantees the bank that you will repay the loan. It's an excellent way to establish credit. Examples of an installment loan would be a car loan, or it could be for furniture or a major appliance. In addition to the above, having a mortgage listed will bring your score even higher.

Throughout this process, always remember:

It takes up to 30 Days for any of these things to get reported and often longer to reflect on your credit history Reports. It feels like a slow process, but hang in there, because it DOES work.

This tedious process can be made much simpler with the automated help of Credit-Aid™ Software www.credit-aid.com. Credit-Aid™ stores your user information to merge into its database of letters, saving you many long hours of letter writing.

A SUMMARY OF YOUR RIGHTS UNDER THE FAIR CREDIT REPORTING ACT

The Federal Fair Credit Reporting Act (FCRA) promotes the accuracy, fairness, and privacy of information in the files of consumer reporting agencies. There are many types of consumer reporting agencies, including credit bureaus and specialty agencies (such as agencies that sell information about check writing histories, medical records, and rental history records). Here is a summary of your major rights under the FCRA. For more information, including information about additional rights, go to www.ftc.gov/credit or write to: Consumer Response Center, Room 130-A, Federal Trade Commission, 600 Pennsylvania Ave. N.W., Washington, D.C. 20580.

You must be told if information in your file has been used against you. Anyone who uses a credit report or another type of consumer report to deny your application for credit, insurance, or employment - or to take another adverse action against you - must tell you, and must give you the name, address, and phone number of the agency that provided the information.

You have the right to know what is in your file. You may request and obtain all the information about you in the files of a consumer reporting agency (your "file disclosure"). You will be required to provide proper identification, which may include your Social Security number. In many cases, the disclosure will be free.

You are entitled to a free file disclosure if:

- A person has taken adverse action against you because of information in your credit report.

- You are the victim of identify theft and place a fraud alert in your file.

- Your file contains inaccurate information as a result of fraud.

- You are on public assistance.

- You are unemployed but expect to apply for employment within 60 days. In addition, by September 2005 all consumers will be entitled to one free disclosure every 12 months upon request from each nationwide credit bureau and from nationwide specialty consumer reporting agencies. See www.ftc.gov/credit for additional information.

You have the right to ask for a credit score. Credit scores are numerical summaries of your credit-worthiness based on information from credit bureaus. You may request a credit score from consumer reporting agencies that create scores or distribute scores used in residential real property loans, but you will have to pay for it. In some mortgage transactions, you will receive credit score information for free from the mortgage lender.

You have the right to dispute incomplete or inaccurate information. If you identify information in your file that is incomplete or inaccurate, and report it to the consumer reporting agency, the agency must investigate unless your dispute is frivolous. See www.ftc.gov/credit for an explanation of dispute procedures.

Consumer reporting agencies must correct or delete inaccurate, incomplete, or unverifiable information. Inaccurate, incomplete or unverifiable information must be removed or corrected, usually within 30 days. However, a consumer reporting agency may continue to report information it has verified as accurate.

Consumer reporting agencies may not report outdated negative information. In most cases, a consumer reporting agency may not report negative information that is more than seven years old, or bankruptcies that are more than 10 years old.

Access to your file is limited. A consumer reporting agency may provide information about you only to people with a valid need -- usually to consider an application with a creditor, insurer, employer, landlord, or other business. The FCRA specifies those with a valid need for access.

You must give your consent for reports to be provided to employers. A consumer reporting agency may not give out information about you to your employer, or a potential employer, without your written consent given to the employer. Written consent generally is not required in the trucking industry. For more information, go to www.ftc.gov/credit .

You may limit "prescreened" offers of credit and insurance you get based on information in your credit report. Unsolicited "prescreened" offers for credit and insurance must include a toll-free phone number you can call if you choose to remove your name and address from the lists these offers are based on. You may opt-out with the nationwide credit bureaus at 1-888-5-OPTOUT (1-888-567-8688).

You may seek damages from violators. If a consumer reporting agency, or, in some cases, a user of consumer reports or a furnisher of information to a consumer reporting agency violates the FCRA, you may be able to sue in state or federal court.

Identity theft victims and active duty military personnel have additional rights. For more information, visit www.ftc.gov/credit.

HOW TO NEGOTIATE FOR A LOWER CREDIT CARD INTEREST (APR)

Most credit card lenders charge anywhere from 0 to 20% in interest (APR). I've seen some particularly creepy banks that charge as much as 35%!

Most people do not realize that you can negotiate with your credit card company for a lower rate, especially if you've had any of your credit cards for a long time.

All you need to do is to call them up to insist on a lower rate. Shoot for 9% to 15%. You'll be surprised at how easy it is to save yourself a lot of money.

Here's how to do it:

1). Start with a credit card that you've had for a long time. One that you have never been late on with payments.

2). Look on the back of the card and dial the customer service number.

3). Start negotiating. Here's a sample script:

Sample Script

You: (Upbeat and polite) "I just got an offer in the mail for a new credit card that has an introductory interest rate of only 6.9%! I don't really want to switch cards, because your service has been wonderful. But even though I've had your card for five years, I'm still paying a 19% rate on my balance. I'm going to have to transfer my balance unless you can lower the interest rate."

Them: (Over the sound of keyboard keys being tapped as your credit and payment history are being examined.) "Hmmm … well, that is the standard rate … but let me see …"

You: "Of course, I understand that, but I can pay a lot less in interest if I transfer my balance. I really need you to reduce the rate to 9% or so."

Them: "Hold on while I check with my supervisor … OK, how about 9.9%?"

You: "No problem." (Now pat yourself on the back for saving some bucks!)

This may not work as well if you're frequently late on your payments and over your head in debt. But it can't hurt to at least ask for an interest rate reduction. If you have a solid track record, handle your obligations and are generally polite, your lender should be willing to offer you a lower rate to keep from losing you to their competition.

4). Keep trying. If you don't get what you want the first time, try to get another customer service rep or a supervisor on the line. They still won't lower the APR? Mark in on your calendar to call them back in a few months.

5). Don't be angry. I have found that I am far more successful in all financial endeavors when being polite. These financial "gatekeepers" have angry people calling them all day long. Imagine what that must be like? Aren't you glad you're not them? I've found that if you're nice and treat them with extra respect, they often return the favor and give you a little extra care.

HOW TO HAVE (AND MAINTAIN) PERFECT CREDIT

Roughly 1% of the population has perfect credit. Perfect credit would mean a FICO score of 850 on Fair Isaac's scale of 300 to 850. Earning such a high credit score does not involve fancy tricks. Folks with such a high credit score all have the following traits in common:

- Between four and six revolving accounts (this means credit cards).

- At least one "installment" trade line (e.g., a mortgage or automobile loan) in good standing.

- Several accounts around 20 years old with a long history of positive use. (To get a score above 800, you need 10 years of positive account history.)

- Around 30 years of credit use.

- No late payments (or other serious account errors) for at least the past seven years.

- Very few credit inquiries (no more than 1-3 in a six-month period).

- No derogatory notations -- collections, bankruptcies, liens, judgments, etc.)

- Debt levels on credit accounts of less than 35% of their overall credit limit.

Now that you know their simple secret, here's what you can do to follow their lead and improve your credit and keep it stellar for life:

See what everyone's saying about you:

Three major credit-reporting agencies are keeping tabs on what you do with your credit and finances. If they're watching, so should you. At least once a year (and a few months before entering into any major loan), review your credit reports from Equifax, Experian and TransUnion. You are entitled to one free copy from each bureau once a year (and more under certain circumstances)

Fix all typos and errors:

Since your credit record spans almost a decade of your borrowing activity, it makes sense that errors sometimes turn up. In fact, a recent study showed that 79% of all credit reports contain errors. This means that your reports have a good chance of having errors. Some common credit-reporting errors include out-of-date addresses, closed accounts being shown as open, credit lines not reported at the correct amount, and erroneous information.

Change your ways, immediately:

Self-inflicted credit wounds (such as a history of late payments, defaults, and general irresponsible behavior) will fade from your record over time. You cannot wipe out accurate information from your credit report. Nor can any firms who offer to do so for a fee. However, it is possible to negotiate removal. Since the most recent behavior on your reports carry more weight than old news, vow that from this day forward you will be a financial upright citizen, and over time your score will grow.

Remember that a credit card is not cash. It represents money you do not have:

Even though you have been approved credit by a bank, a store, etc (Visa, MasterCard, Sears, Kmart, etc.) to borrow thousands of dollars, you don't actually have thousands of dollars to spend, which leads nicely to the next rule...

Ignore anyone's rules on what should be an "acceptable" amount of debt:

Your debt-to-income ratio is the measure of how much debt you carry to how much money (after taxes) you have coming in. In the world of lending, it is acceptable to carry 25% of your income in debt. That ratio is still very high. You might want to consider trying to keep your debt (including car loans)to 15% or less of your after-tax income.

In summary:

Based on the above information, you can see the tricks to keeping your credit score high. Just keep your spending under control, pay your bills on time, and don't apply for credit too often. Follow those rules and your credit score will start to rise.

STARTING A CREDIT REPAIR BUSINESS

So many mortgage brokers and entrepreneurs call and write asking how to start a credit repair business. I decided to add this info into our book.

Starting a credit repair business is very simple and your timing couldn't be any better for this lucrative business opportunity. Nearly 80 million Americans have poor credit. Many do not understand the credit reporting system and will gladly pay good money for someone to help them with their credit. Why shouldn't that be you?

A credit repair business

- Is a recession-proof

- Excels during tough economic times

- Is easy to run from your home

- Can make you money immediately

- Is easy to start with very little investment

- Pays for itself after just a few clients

- Is a great supplement to your existing business and does a service for the community.

Credit repair brings in new streams of revenue and passive income. Mortgage brokers, loan officers, real estate agents and auto dealers use credit repair to generate new leads and close more loans. Many entrepreneurs use credit repair as an affordable home business that can earn them an additional $5000- $10,000 a month and more.

Learning the basics of credit repair enables you to start a new business immediately. It's something you can easily do in your home or office, because all you need is a computer, a mouse and a printer.

Helping others repair their credit history and have a fresh new head start on life is very rewarding. While it's true that consumers can do this very same work themselves, most people don't want to deal with the aggravation of talking to credit bureaus to correct mistakes, handle disputes or negotiate with creditors. This is where you come in to handle all that for them.

Here are the steps to get started with a credit repair business

1. GET A COPY OF YOUR OWN CREDIT REPORT TO STUDY.

    You are entitled to one free copy a year, and there are three major credit bureaus to see reports from: Equifax, Experian and Trans-Union.

2. LEARN AS MUCH AS YOU CAN ABOUT THE CREDIT REPORTING SYSTEM.

    We offer a copy of the Fair Credit Reporting Act right on our site. We also offer a free eBook with credit repair tips with every purchase of our credit-aid software. You can also download guides at the FTC web site. Also see our blogs and other resources in the last chapter.

3. UNDERSTAND YOUR ROLE IN THE PROCESS

    Once you obtain your clients credit reports, you can then work with that client to correct any mistakes, acting as the intermediary between them and the credit bureau or creditor.

4. UNDERSTAND WHAT YOU ARE SELLING AND TAKE CARE IN WHAT YOU PROMISE

    A credit repair company cannot "erase" negative items that are accurate and have been present on a credit report for less than seven years. However, many accurate but negative items can be removed with a bit of finesse if you learn the right negotiating tactics and approach the creditors and collection agencies in the proper manner. Here's the good news: 79% of all credit reports contain errors. This means that MOST credit reports contain errors. Those errors come off very easily with a few clicks of your mouse. Simply removing errors will improve a score almost immediately. Once you've accomplished that, you can further enhance a credit report by negotiating the remaining negative items.

5.   WORK SMART AND MINIMIZE TIME SPENT WORKING

The most common mistake more entrepreneurs make is in managing their time poorly. Time spent creating dispute letters and handling paperwork can eat up hundreds of hours and drop your hourly earnings very low. This is where software comes in handy. It can help you to work "smart" by saving you hundreds of hours by automating the process and giving you more off-time to enjoy your success.

6.   PROMOTE AND MARKET YOUR BUSINESS

Now that you have everything in place, it's time to start promoting and marketing your credit consulting business. You might call local credit repair businesses to get an idea of the services they offer and the types of fees associated with these services. In our own PRO software we give a breakdown of suggested fees. Some credit repair specialists don't charge fees at all. For mortgage brokers and auto dealers the reward can be greater in generating leads and closing more loans. Go through all the information you can find, decide on your fees and services, and get ready to advertise.

It's easy to create credit repair business flyers and business cards, either professionally or on your home computer. On the flyers, give a brief description about your services and contact information. Remember. Less is more. Post these flyers everywhere you can. You may also want to place small ads for your services in local newspapers, church newsletters, periodicals and with local merchants who deal with financing: mortgage brokers, real estate agents, auto dealers, etc.

Offer friends and family your credit repair counseling services for free, and then ask them for a letter of recommendation. This will quickly help to build your client base. Word of mouth is the very best kind of advertising.

You may want to consider giving credit repair and debt seminars and classes to help people to help themselves before they are too far in debt. Perhaps you might want to give talks at high schools and colleges about ways to stay out of debt. The students will go home with the information you have given them, and your business card or brochure, and tell their parents, who could end up as your next clients.

7.   START SMALL AND WORK OUT KINKS BEFORE EXPANDING TOO QUICKLY

As a credit consultant, you should start to build your business locally before expanding too fast or going to the internet. If you build your credibility early, when you branch out, you will have experience and a history of customer satisfaction to back you up.

Stay honest with your clients. You are providing them with a very important service. They must trust you and your business. Credit repair can be confusing to many. Reassure and give them the information they want. This will enhance your credibility and increase your credit repair business well into the future.

Running a credit repair business can be made simpler with the help of Software www.creditaidpro.com Credit repair software stores your client information to merge into its database of letters, saving you many long hours of letter writing.

WHAT IS THE BEST CREDIT REPAIR SOFTWARE?

It's Credit-Aid Software of Course! Credit-Aid Software automates the process of cleaning up your credit and boosting your Credit score. It's 100% legal and written by attorneys to use the credit repair system to your advantage. Order free credit reports, remove errors, generate letters, negotiate with creditors, track your finances and keep it all organized.

*Credit-Aid Software is a "stand-alone" easy-to-use software program that you install and run on your own computer. Your user data is safely encrypted and remains stored only on your computer and is not transmitted over the Internet.

Download it right now at www.credit-aid.com

View our professional software at www.creditaidpro.com

Habla Espanol? Credit-Aid is available in Spanish at www.Ayuda-Credito.com

MORE RESOURCES

For more information about credit repair, our software, earning money as an affiliate, obtaining credit "scores" or to start a credit repair home business, please visit our website, forum and blog.

www.credit-aid.com
www.creditaidpro.com
www.ayuda-credit-.com
www.the-credit-repair-blog
www.creditandfinance101.com